Introduction

Over 175 million people visit a zoo each year.

There are over 350 zoos in the United States.

The largest zoo is the Berlin Zoological Gardens, which has 19,500 individual animals!

 is for Apes.

There are many different kinds of apes found at zoo, these include chimpanzees, gorillas, orangutans, and gibbons.

Apes are not monkeys, they are much larger and do not have tails.

My First Book about the Alphabet of Zoo Animals

Amazing Animal Books
Children's Picture Books

By Molly Davidson

Mendon Cottage Books

JD-Biz Publishing

Read More Amazing Animal Books

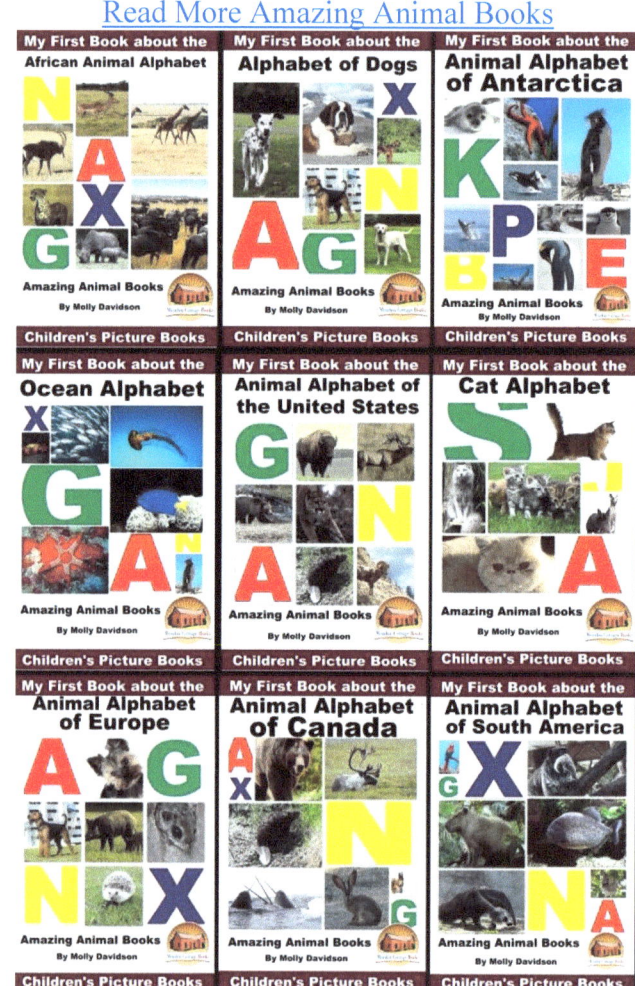

Purchase at Amazon.com

Download Free Books!
http://MendonCottageBooks.com

 is for a Blue & Yellow Macaw.

Blue and yellow macaws are the 6th most common animal found at the zoo.

Macaws' beaks are so strong they can crush a human knuckle with one crack.

Macaws can live for over 50 years in the wild and even longer if they are kept in a zoo.

B is also for a Boa Constrictor.

Boa means "large serpent" in Latin and it is the 9th most common animal found at a zoo.

The largest boa in a zoo was named Fluffy. She died in 2010, and weighed 300 pounds and was 24 feet long.

C is for a Crocodile.

Crocodiles do not stop growing until they die.

Lolong is the longest crocodile ever to be in a zoo; he was 20 1/4 feet long and weighed 2,370 pounds when he died in 2013.

D is for a Dolphin.

Dolphins do not drink saltwater; they get the water they need from the fish they eat.

They are very smart and are easily trained, giving some amazing shows to zoo visitors.

 **is for an Elephant.**

An elephant's skin is so sensitive it can feel a fly landing on it.

Boy elephants can weigh up to 15,000 pounds.

Many zoos have trained elephants that do tricks for the zoo visitors.

E is also for an Emu.

An emu is the 10th most common animal found at the zoo.

When an emu runs, their stride can be up to 9 feet long.

They are great swimmers, and love ponds and lakes.

F

is for a Flamingo.

Many of the World's largest zoos have successfully hatched over 450 flamingo chicks, helping keep them from extinction.

Standing on one leg really is the most comfortable position for a flamingo.

G is for a Giraffe.

Giraffes are the 8th most common animal found at a zoo.

They have a black tongue, which helps it from getting sunburned.

G is also for a Giant Panda.

Giant pandas were almost extinct in the 1960's, but with help from many zoos and lots of research, over 300 baby pandas have now been born in zoos, and hundreds more in the wild.

They can eat up to 36 lbs of bamboo per day, to eat that much takes them about 12 hours.

H

 is for a Hippopotamus.

Hippos love water but they cannot swim, instead they just push their toes off the bottom of the pond or river, slowing walking through the water.

Adult hippopotamuses can hold their breath underwater for up to 30 minutes.

I is for an Iguana.

Iguanas can live in dry deserts or tropical rainforests, where they are fabulous swimmers.

Iguanas can have a totally different color of skin in the shade than in the sun.

Iguanas get rid of extra salt through their nose.

 **is for a Jaguar.**

Jaguars are the third largest cat, behind lions and tigers, weighing up to 250 pounds.

They live in trees that are close to water, where they love to go swimming and catch fish to eat.

Baby cubs can start hunting on their own by the time they are 15 - 18 months old.

 **is for a Kangaroo.**

Kangaroos can jump up to 35 miles per hour, but cannot walk backwards.

Mothers are called does, and they have a pouch on their front where their tiny baby, called a joey, lives until it is ready to survive in the outside World.

L is for a Lion.

Lions are the second most popular animal found at a zoo.

The adult women, called lionesses, do almost all the hunting for the group, called a pride.

M  is for a Meerkat.

Meerkats are the fifth most popular animal found at a zoo.

Timon, a character in the movie <u>The Lion King</u>, was based on a meerkat in the San Diego Zoo.

 is for a Nubian Ibex.

Nubian ibex are a species of wild goat, which is also the fourth most common animal at a zoo.

Both the boys and the girls have horns that curve backwards, the boys can grow as long as 48 inches.

 **is for an Otter.**

Otters can close their nose and ears so they can swim and dive underwater.

Otters were not kept at zoos until the 1950's.

They have 100,000 hairs in the space of a postage stamp, which helps keep them warm.

P is for a Peafowl.

Probably every zoo in America has peafowl, making them the 8th most common zoo animal.

Only the boys have brightly colored feathers which they spread out wide to attract girls.

P is also for a Penguin.

There are 17 different species of penguin, which all live in the southern hemisphere.

All penguins eat fish, and they are fed twice a day herring, smelt, and capelin at zoos.

Penguins cannot fly; they have flippers which make them great underwater swimmers and hunters.

R is for a Ring-Tailed Lemur.

Ring-tailed lemurs are the third most common animal found at a zoo, the most popular primate.

Their striped tails help them find one another in the forests of Madagascar, where they live.

R is also for a Rhinoceros.

Even though rhinos can weigh up to 5,000 pounds they can run up to 40 miles per hour.

Black rhinos are now totally extinct in the wild and are only found in zoos, due to over hunting for their horns.

S is for a Sun Bear.

Sun bears are the seventh most common animal found at a zoo, the only bear in the top ten.

They live in tropical climates and do not hibernate, since there is no freezing winter.

S is also for a Secretary Bird.

Secretary birds stand over 4 feet tall, and spend their days on the ground, but fly high into the acacia trees at night.

T is for a Tiger.

The number one most common animal found at a zoo is the tiger.

They can kill prey that is 4 times larger than them.

Tigers can eat 20 pounds of meat per day, and up to 100 pounds in one meal.

U is for an Ursus Maritimus, the scientific name for a Polar Bear.

Polar bears have such thick fur to help stay warm in their freezing climate that they sometimes over heat and have to jump in the water to cool off.

V  is for a Vulture.

Many species of vultures were becoming endangered due to eating poisoned meat of dead animals, until many zoos stepped in to help.

They can carry meat up to one-third of their body weight to their nests.

W is for a Wolf.

Wolves will travel hundreds of miles in search of food.

Many wolves found in zoos are donated by regular citizens who cannot keep them as a pet anymore.

 **is for a Zebra.**

Every zebra has a different stripe pattern.

Zebras that live in the Serengeti eat the top of grass, leaving the bottom for smaller animals.

They have a pad of fat which helps keep their mane standing straight up.

Conclusion

I hope you have enjoyed reading this book about many of the amazing animals you can find in a zoo.

One more fact, over $16 billion is donated to zoos each year to help animals.

Download Free Books!

http://MendonCottageBooks.com

Horses For Kids
Amazing Animal Books For Young Readers
By John and Annalee Davidson

Ponies For Kids
Mendon Cottage Books
Amazing Animal Books For young Readers
Rachel Smith

Ten Amazing Horses For Kids
Nature Books for Kids
JD-Biz Publishing
K. Bennett

Akhal-Teke "The Golden Horse of the desert" For Kids
Nature Books for Kids
JD-Biz Publishing
K. Bennett

Suffolk-Punch "The Gentle Giant" For Kids
Nature Books for Kids
JD-Biz Publishing
K. Bennett

Shires "The great Horse" For Kids
Nature Books for Kids
JD-Biz Publishing
K. Bennett

Colonial Spanish "Horse of the Americas" For Kids
Nature Books for Kids
JD-Biz Publishing
K. Bennett

Canadian "The Little Iron Horse" For Kids
Nature Books for Kids
JD-Biz Publishing
K. Bennett

Cleveland Bays "History and Future" Horses For Kids
Nature Books for Kids
JD-Biz Publishing
K. Bennett

Top Ten Dog Breeds For Kids
Amazing Animal Books For Young Readers
Kisha Bennett & John Davidson

German Shepherds
Dog Books for Kids
K. Bennett

Bulldogs
Dog Books for Kids
K. Bennett

Dachshund
Dog Books for Kids
K. Bennett

Poodles
Dog Books for Kids
K. Bennett

Labrador Retrievers
Dog Books for Kids
K. Bennett

Rottweilers
Dog Books for Kids
K. Bennett

Boxers
Dog Books for Kids
K. Bennett

Golden Retrievers
Dog Books for Kids
K. Bennett

Puppies
Dog Books For Kids
Amazing Animal Books
By John Davidson

Beagles
Dog Books for Kids
K. Bennett

Yorkshire Terriers
Dog Books for Kids
K. Bennett

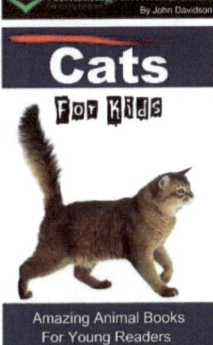

Dogs Top Ten Dog Breeds For Kids
Amazing Animal Books For Young Readers
Zahra Jazeel & John Davidson

Cats For Kids
Amazing Animal Books For Young Readers
K. Bennett & John Davidson

Foxes For Kids
Amazing Animal Books For Young Readers
Zahra Jazeel & John Davidson

Wolves For Kids
Amazing Animal Books For Young Readers
By John Davidson and Virginia Fidler

Our books are available at

1. Amazon.com

2. Barnes and Noble

3. Itunes

4. Kobo

5. Smashwords

6. Google Play Books

Download Free Books!
http://MendonCottageBooks.com

Publisher

JD-Biz Corp

P O Box 374

Mendon, Utah 84325

http://www.jd-biz.com/

www.ingramcontent.com/pod-product-compliance
Lightning Source LLC
Chambersburg PA
CBHW050848290526
45792CB00002B/573